Blackout! Cities in Darkness

Therese DeAngelis
AR B.L.: 7.7
Points: 1.0

MG

Blackout!

Cities in Darkness

Therese De Angelis

Enslow Publishers, Inc.

40 Industrial Road   PO Box 38
Box 398   Aldershot
Berkeley Heights, NJ 07922   Hants GU12 6BP
USA   UK

http://www.enslow.com

This book is dedicated to Dr. Jane E. Phillips, my good friend and "cheering section" for the past 25 years. Thanks for everything, P.

Library of Congress Cataloging-in-Publication Data

De Angelis, Therese.
    Blackout! : cities in darkness / Therese De Angelis.
        p. cm. — (American disasters)
    Summary: Reviews the causes and effects of some major blackouts, from the
1965 power outage that affected much of New England to the 2001 rolling blackouts in California, focusing on the 1977 blackout in New York City that lasted over
twenty-five hours.
    Includes bibliographical references and index.
    ISBN 0-7660-2110-6
    1. Electric power failures—United States—Juvenile literature. [1. Electric power
failures. 2. Power resources.]   I. Title. II. Series.
TK3091.D353 2003
333.793'2—dc21

                            2002009554

Printed in the United States of America

10 9 8 7 6 5 4 3 2 1

To Our Readers: We have done our best to make sure all Internet Addresses in this book were active and appropriate when we went to press. However, the author and the publisher have no control over and assume no liability for the material available on those Internet sites or on other Web sites they may link to. Any comments or suggestions can be sent by e-mail to comments@enslow.com or to the address on the back cover.

Illustration Credits: AP/Wide World Photos, pp. 4, 7, 11, 13, 15, 16, 17, 18, 21, 26, 29, 30, 31, 33, 35, 37, 39, 40; Cary Herz/The Newark Star-Ledger Photo Library, p. 8; © Olivier Rebbot/Contact Press Images, pp. 9, 24.

Cover Illustration: AP/Wide World Photos.

Contents

An open fire hydrant provides some relief for this New Yorker during the heat wave that gripped the city in July 1977.

CHAPTER 1

Terror in the Darkness

Wednesday, July 13, 1977, was a hot, humid day in New York City. For several weeks, the entire region had been in the midst of a terrible heat wave, and this day was no different. Some residents stayed in their air-conditioned homes to escape the heat. Others went out to theaters or restaurants. Even after the sun went down that evening, many people were still seeking relief from the 90-degree heat. Most were unaware that outside, up in the night sky, storm clouds were gathering.

Later that night, when the rain finally came, it filled the sky with claps of thunder and vivid streaks of lightning. Suddenly, at 9:34 P.M., the entire city of New York was plunged into blackness. The effect was eerie. The blazing Broadway lights and glowing skyscrapers of Manhattan were snuffed out. The busy hum of air conditioners and refrigerators abruptly stopped.

Elevators, subways, and trains all shut down. Traffic lights blinked out. Hospital equipment also shut down—including respirators, which help patients breathe. Even though the hospitals had emergency power sources, at least two of them failed.

Restaurant and theater patrons engulfed in darkness tried to continue by candlelight. Kennedy International and LaGuardia airports both went dark, as did the New York Stock Exchange. At Shea Stadium in Queens, the blackout interrupted a baseball game between the New York Mets and Chicago Cubs. In order to take people's minds off of the heat, stadium organist Jane Jarvis played "White Christmas."[1]

At first it seemed that New Yorkers would handle the massive blackout calmly and with good humor, as they had done during a previous blackout in 1965. Neighbors knocked on each other's doors to see if they were okay. Civilians with flashlights joined policemen on the highways and streets to help direct traffic. On Coney Island, sixteen bystanders helped turn the 150-foot-high "Wonder Wheel" by hand in order to allow the ride's passengers to safely reach the ground.[2]

In Grand Central Terminal, all trains had shut down, leaving many commuters stranded. Some politely stood by phone booths and held flashlights so that others could see to dial home and let their families know they were safe. In a subway tunnel at Broadway and 19th Street, Transit Authority Police Officer Thomas Duffey guided 1,500 passengers out of a train without incident.[3]

Within minutes after the blackout began, however, other parts of the city erupted in violence. On the Upper West Side, in East Harlem, and in downtown Brooklyn,

*T*hese stranded commuters relax on the floor of Grand Central Station in the early hours of July 14, 1977.

mobs of looters under the cover of darkness began smashing store windows. "It was almost as if they came out of the air," one store owner said.[4] The sounds of shattering glass, wailing alarms, and clanging trash cans echoed throughout the city. Looters carried off armloads of groceries, clothing, jewelry, liquor, sporting goods, and even appliances and furniture.

At first, the atmosphere around the looting was calm—almost businesslike. "The only thing that really surprised me was that it was quite orderly," one of the looters later said. Aubrey Edmonds, who lived and worked in the Bushwick section of Brooklyn, watched as the looting began. "It was started by twenty-one to thirty-year-olds who knew what to get and where to get it," he recalled. "This was their business." On Bushwick's Utica Avenue, one looter pulled up to a store in a thirty-eight-foot moving van.[5]

As the night wore on, however, this relative calm soon gave way to hysteria. "People [began] running around like crazy, like a pack of wild dogs," one witness remembered. "They started massing together to yank down the gates. All up and down Flatbush Avenue police cars were zooming up and down, but they had no effect. . . . People were taking TVs, washing machines; the stuff too heavy to carry they just abandoned in the street."[6]

As vandals set fire to trash in waste cans, thousands of

Stranded visitors play cards by candlelight at the Roosevelt Hotel during the 1977 blackout.

*L*ooters frantically wrestle with one another during the 1977 blackout.

nervous residents throughout the city triggered fire alarms. Fire departments had no choice but to respond to each one, and they were soon overwhelmed.

Police stations were barraged with 911 emergency calls reporting muggings, purse-snatchings, shootings, and vandalism. Some officers were confronted with angry crowds hurling bricks, rocks, and bottles. The situation became so dangerous that New York Governor Hugh Carey ordered state police into the city to help local law enforcement.

Mayor Abraham Beame was in the borough of the Bronx when the blackout struck. He immediately rushed to City Hall, where he ordered all of the city's commissioners to meet him. In a building lit only by candles, the mayor ordered all of the city's fire and prison officers to report to work at once. Despite this order, about 10,000 of the city's 25,000 officers and supervisors never showed up.[7]

One of the worst-hit areas was the Fulton Street shopping district in Brooklyn. Entire storefronts were torn away and the stores looted. At least four police officers were injured in Brooklyn and three were hurt in Harlem. Even the state police seemed to do little good. There were so many lawbreakers that police could not arrest them quickly enough. In Brooklyn, officers bringing suspects to the central booking office on 301 Gold Street simply left them there without explanation and returned to the streets immediately.[8] Hundreds of looters were crammed into cells meant to hold just a few prisoners.

During the rampage, desperate store owners tried to protect their businesses. Some carried guns to ward off looters, but most were unsuccessful. Carl Neufeld, the owner of Ace Pontiac Showroom in the South Bronx, could do nothing as looters smashed his steel door and plate-glass windows. They made off with about fifty new cars, worth a total of $250,000.[9] A clothing store owner in the Bushwick section of Brooklyn stood by helplessly, with tears in his eyes, as more than a hundred people emptied his shop of merchandise. "This is the end of Broadway in Brooklyn," he said. He lost $200,000.[10]

The worst crime sprees that night occurred between midnight and 4:00 A.M. in areas of Brooklyn such as Williamsburg and Bushwick. There, the mayhem grew potentially deadly. When John & Al's Sports at 297 Broadway was pillaged, vandals made off with armloads of guns and thousands of rounds of ammunition. Police officers later reported being targeted by snipers. A store set on fire at Broadway and Gates Avenue in Bushwick exploded as firefighters tried to extinguish the flames. Twenty-two of them were injured.[11]

New York City Mayor Abe Beame ordered all of the city's fire and prison officers to immediately report to work after the blackout struck.

Consolidated Edison (Con Ed), one of the country's largest public utility companies, served millions of customers in the city and in New York's Westchester County. Throughout the night, the company struggled to restore power to the area. Although city officials, police, firefighters, and most residents hoped that daylight would restore calm, the bedlam continued into Thursday. Amazingly, in Brooklyn and East Harlem, the looting seemed to intensify during daylight hours. Shopkeepers were terrified of what might happen if the city was still without electricity at sundown. Others wondered whether even restoring the power would stem the tide of crime.

CHAPTER 2

A City in Distress

The blackout of 1977 was not the first time New York City experienced such a crisis. On November 9, 1965, the entire northeast—eight states and parts of Canada—went dark for more than twelve hours. The outage began at 5:27 P.M. in Queenston, Ontario, when an overloaded transmission relay (a remote-control switch for electrical circuits) shut off power to the city of Toronto. Other power companies connected to the station were unable to take up the slack, and the failure triggered a massive, cascading blackout.

Within thirty minutes, the blackout spread south across 80,000 square miles. New Hampshire, Vermont, Massachusetts, Connecticut, Rhode Island, New York, and parts of New Jersey and Pennsylvania were affected. Thirty million Canadians and Americans were without power. In New York City, four million homes went dark and as many as 800,000 people were stranded in subway cars for hours. By 6:58 A.M. on November 10, power was restored citywide.

One of the biggest differences between the Great Northeast Blackout of 1965 (as it became known) and the July 1977 outage was the way in which New Yorkers handled each crisis. In 1965, despite confusion and fear, little vandalism occurred. Residents helped direct traffic and rescue stranded subway passengers. Neighbors knocked

A darkened New York City skyline is pictured here during a blackout that took place on November 9, 1965. Buildings that are lit had emergency power generators.

on one another's doors to make sure they had candles, batteries, flashlights, and radios.[1] Many who lived through the blackout had fond memories of getting to know people whom they had been too busy to meet when the electricity was on.

After the 1965 blackout, backup and safety measures were put in place so that an entire grid could not be shut down by a single equipment failure. City governments along the northeast coast also installed new backup lighting systems and more power generators. They established rules requiring that emergency systems be tested regularly to be sure they were functioning properly. Most people believed that these measures would prevent a widespread blackout from occurring again.

The time between the blackouts of 1965 and 1977 was one of tremendous upheaval in New York City and across the country. Great changes took place in politics, fashion, and lifestyle, as people began to question long-held beliefs. Many women turned away from their more traditional roles as wives and mothers to pursue professional careers. Some women and men chose to live in communes—rural communities where people shared all their wealth and property. People lived their lives the way they chose. Anything seemed possible.

This wealth of possibilities was reflected in popular culture. Many new forms of music, for example, blossomed in the 1970s. Punk-rock pioneers like the Ramones began playing regularly in the New York Bowery club CBGBs, along with new wave acts like Blondie. In April

1977, the legendary nightclub Studio 54 opened. For three years until it closed in 1980, the glittery hot spot was the hub for a wildly popular new dance style—disco—launched by the box-office hit *Saturday Night Fever* in 1977. Another smash hit that summer was the special-effects wonder *Star Wars.* "Betcha can't see it just once," ads dared moviegoers.

The lights of Broadway also seemed to burn brighter during the 1970s. The musical *A Chorus Line* premiered at the Shubert Theater on July 25, 1975. When it closed fifteen years later, after 6,137 performances, it was the longest-running musical

*D*eborah Harry, lead singer of Blondie, is pictured here in March 1980. Many punk and new wave bands like Blondie got their start performing at New York clubs in the mid-1970s.

in history. The late-night TV variety show *Saturday Night Live*, still broadcast out of New York City, also premiered in 1975.

The Manhattan skyline underwent a dramatic change in 1973, when the Twin Towers of the World Trade Center were completed. When they opened to the public the following spring, the Twin Towers were the tallest buildings

*M*ark Hamill, Carrie Fisher, and Harrison Ford (left to right) star as Luke Skywalker, Princess Leia, and Han Solo, respectively, in a scene from the blockbuster film *Star Wars*, which premiered in the summer of 1977.

in the world. During the construction of the 110-story buildings, French stuntman Philippe Petit walked a tightrope strung between the towers. Later, in May 1977, a man named George Willig climbed up the side of one of the towers. He was arrested at the top and fined $1.10— one penny for each floor of the building.[2]

In October 1976 the New York Yankees closed a dramatic postseason series against the Kansas City Royals with a walk-off home run from first baseman Chris Chambliss in the deciding fifth game. The playoff victory vaulted the Yanks into the World Series for the first time in twelve years. This same year, New York led a dazzling

U.S. bicentennial celebration with Operation Sail. A thrilling procession of square-riggers (tall-masted ships) from around the world sailed majestically through New York Harbor.

But New York City, along with the rest of the country, also faced many struggles during the 1970s. In 1973, the U.S. pulled out of a lengthy war in Vietnam, but the war left the nation with deep emotional scars. Around this same time, the Watergate scandal came to light. The scandal

French aerialist Philippe Petit walks a tightrope strung between the not-yet-completed Twin Towers of the World Trade Center on August 7, 1974.

centered on an illegal break-in at the headquarters of the Democratic National Committee in 1972. As a result of this crime, President Richard Nixon was forced to resign from office in disgrace in 1974.

The 1970s were also trying times for the country economically. In 1973, an energy crisis began in the United States when the Organization of Petroleum Exporting Countries (OPEC) decided to cut production and reduce exports of oil. This led to long lines and soaring prices at gas stations. The country was also experiencing terrible inflation (rising prices for items) and a high rate of unemployment.

By the early 1970s, the federal government had severely cut back on financial aid to New York City. Corporations

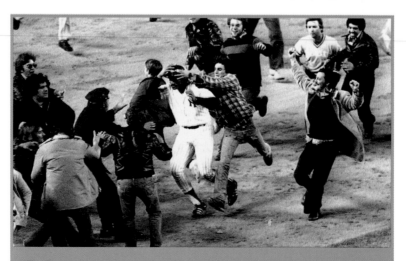

New York Yankees first baseman Chris Chambliss is mobbed by fans on the field of Yankee Stadium as he rounds the bases after hitting his playoff–game-winning home run on October 14, 1976.

that once based their businesses in the city began moving out, as did many thousands of middle-class residents. Before long, New York City was no longer taking in enough revenue to pay its bills. It had exceeded its own budget and spent more money than it had collected, mainly for social programs such as welfare.

By 1975, New York City was broke. Private banks that had loaned the city millions of dollars refused to lend any more until it repaid them the $6 billion it already owed. The city government turned to the federal government for financial help, but on October 29, President Gerald Ford said he would not guarantee New York's loans. This prompted the *New York Daily News* to print a story with the now-famous headline: "Ford to City: Drop Dead."[3] (Eventually, the federal government did give the city loan guarantees that enabled it to survive the crisis.)

Money problems were not the only difficulty facing New York City during the 1970s. The crime rate was soaring, too. Reports of widespread corruption in the city's police department also surfaced in 1972. A series of strikes by garbage collectors, hospital physicians, and police officers demoralized the city.

In the South Bronx, fires burned almost constantly, set by angry, unemployed people in one of the poorest sections of New York. Most of these sections of the city had been "redlined"—which meant that banks refused to give loans to people in these neighborhoods (in effect, drawing a "red line" around them on a map). This made it nearly impossible for most poor people to improve their quality of life.

Terrorism was also on the minds of many New Yorkers during this time. In January 1975, four people were killed when a bomb exploded in Fraunces Tavern, a historic building in lower Manhattan. The incident was one of forty-nine bombings between 1974 and 1977 attributed to the Puerto Rican nationalist group FALN. In December 1975, a bomb planted by Croatian terrorists in New York's LaGuardia Airport killed eleven people and injured seventy-five others. The following September, Croatian terrorists hijacked TWA Flight 355, carrying eighty-six passengers from New York to Chicago, and had it flown to France.[4]

In July 1976, New York City began experiencing another kind of terror. A serial murderer calling himself "Son of Sam" stalked young couples parked in cars in the city's "lovers' lanes." He fatally shot six people and wounded seven others. As the murders continued, teenagers and young couples avoided being out after dark. So terrifying were the murder reports that when it was publicized that the first few victims had brown hair, many young women began wearing blonde wigs.[5]

In January 1977, Son of Sam sent a letter to Captain Joseph Borelli, who was heading the investigation into the serial murders. "I am the Monster," the killer wrote. "I love to hunt. Prowling the streets looking for fair game. . . . The women of Queens are prettyist [sic] of all." Other letters were sent to newspaper columnists. "Sam . . .

*P*olice escort "Son of Sam," David Berkowitz, outside of Brooklyn's 84th precinct shortly after his arrest on August 11, 1977.

won't let me stop killing until he gets his fill of blood," he wrote to *Daily News* columnist Jimmy Breslin.[6]

Son of Sam turned out to be a twenty-four-year-old Yonkers postal clerk named David Berkowitz—but he would not be captured until almost a month after the blackout. So at the time the blackout struck, fear of the serial killer intensified.

Clearly, the 1977 blackout was a brutal blow to a city that was already staggering under the weight of many serious problems. When the lights went out on July 13, 1977, some may have wondered if they would ever come back on again.

CHAPTER 3

The Long, Dark Hours

When New York City went dark on July 13, 1977, many were not aware of how widespread the blackout was. They soon found out, however, when they heard the sounds of glass breaking and metal gates being torn from storefronts. When daylight arrived, the looting did not stop, even though there was little left to steal or smash.

"They're grabbing anything now," said one police officer in East Harlem the next morning, as he drove through trash-strewn streets.[1] "They were like bluefish in a feeding frenzy," Captain Driscoll of the 81st Precinct in Bedford-Stuyvesant later said. "The strongest feeling I had was one of disbelief. I've seen looting before, but this was total devastation. Smashing, burning . . . as if they'd gone crazy."[2]

Some attributed the mayhem that occurred in the city's poorer sections to the residents' overwhelming feelings of frustration and anger. These New Yorkers, many argued, lived in poverty in a city that had cut back on the few services that helped them. They watched helplessly as crime became a part of everyday life. A great number had also lost their jobs. Robert Anazagasti was director of the East Harlem Community Corporation, a social service agency, when the blackout struck. "When you are hungry," he said, "and you haven't worked in a long time [and] the opportunity presents itself, you know it's wrong, but you take it." Anazagasti and his employees drove through East Harlem on July 14 with bullhorns, pleading with residents to remain calm. "Don't give your community a black eye by destroying what is yours," they said.[3]

Others were not so understanding. A sports shop owner in Brooklyn stood with a high-powered rifle near his store and vowed to defend it. "God knows I don't want to shoot anybody, but I can't allow them to just carry my store away."[4] A Brooklyn ice-cream shop owner reacted, as did many others, with disgust. "They're crazy," he said of the looters. "They're animals. They should be put in jail— and throw the key away."[5]

Michael Alesi is the current owner of the Tom, Dick, and Harry shoe store in Bushwick, which was the most heavily vandalized area of the city. His father owned the business in 1977. "At that time we had iron gates," Alesi recalled in 1997. "[The vandals] must have pulled the gates off with a car. Forget about it. We must have had about a quarter of a million dollars in sneakers stolen from us."[6]

Many people who did not participate in the chaos were stunned to witness the ransacking of their own

S hortly after the blackout struck New York City, crowds of looters began tearing down the security gates that protected storefronts.

neighborhoods. One teenager remembered how the experience affected her:

> I remember sitting on my stoop with a boyfriend when all of the lights faded to black. I sat there, afraid to move. I heard screaming, then laughing. From that point on, all I could see were shadows of people running back and forth in the dark. I watched as our neighborhood was destroyed by the people that lived in it. They wrecked and looted our supermarkets, our shopping centers, our clothing stores and department stores. . . . People had gotten hurt. . . . I remember thinking, why would they do this here? Where we live? . . .[7]

"A lot of people didn't know what was going on," one looter explained, "but when they saw all the looting, they [joined in]. You see other people jump into a store and you [say], 'I'm going too. I'm going in there and getting . . . something too.'" Another looter explained her actions this way: "Everybody was doing it and it was free. I was right next door. . . . I did it for the fun of it."[8]

Many were simply too busy to think about what caused the rioting. At city hospitals, the blackout triggered emergency power systems meant to keep respirators and other life-support equipment running. But about forty minutes after the city went dark, the backup power failed at Bellevue Hospital. Respirators for fifteen patients stopped working, so doctors and nurses squeezed airbags by hand to help patients breathe.[9] After many hours passed without power, however, officials had to find other means to help patients. They hooked up older-model respirators to portable generators that operated on gasoline. When they ran out of gas, Dr. Henry Frey siphoned more from the tank of his car.[10]

Dr. Robert Dawe was working at St. Luke's Hospital near Columbia University when the blackout hit. Almost immediately, a steady stream of patients entered the emergency room with what would become familiar complaints. "We treated 10 or 11 people with stab wounds and [more than] 100 with lacerations [torn and ragged wounds] from putting their hands through glass windows or from having pieces of glass fall on them," he said. "It was a violent night. You could hear the windows being smashed along Broadway."[11] At the Brooklyn Jewish Hospital and Medical Center, physicians and nurses

Firefighters battle a storefront inferno in the Bronx on July 14, 1977.

treated patients in the parking lot, which was lit by high-intensity spotlights powered by local fire department generators. "It's like wartime and we're at the battle-front," nurse William Dickenson said. "This is ten times worse than the last blackout. . . . [Patients] say they cut themselves on bottles, but it's the looting and the smashing of windows that's cutting them up."[12]

On the streets, police officers and firefighters were facing horrifying conditions. "We were scared to death," a young city policeman recalled. "Anyone who says he was not is lying—but worse than that, the blue [police officer's] uniform didn't mean a thing [to the looters]."[13]

On Utica Avenue in Crown Heights, police estimated that thousands of people were crammed into a narrow street five blocks long. Ultimately, there were simply too many looters and not enough police officers. "We were just pests," said Sergeant O'Houlihan of the 73rd Precinct in Brownsville. "We were just something to get around so they could get at the goods."[14]

Despite the mayhem, some New Yorkers managed to enjoy themselves. At Park Avenue and 79th Street on Manhattan's East Side, a young man directed traffic with the gusto of a bullfighter. The man wore a cape and held a flare in one hand and a flashlight in the other. Drivers who ignored him were met with a loud, echoing command to "Stop!" He explained that he had seen a few near-accidents and decided to step in. "I thought I'd stop and help them out a little," he said. "They stop when I tell them. They go when I tell them."[15]

Other city residents were also able to maintain a sense of humor despite the blackout. One woman had been walking her dog on the Upper East Side when the lights went out. Somewhere in the darkness, a man whistled at her and yelled "Hey, beautiful!"

"How can you tell?" the woman replied.[16]

CHAPTER 4

Learning Lessons

Con Ed was unable to restore power to New York City until 10:40 P.M. on July 14—more than twenty-five hours after the blackout began. By then, huge sections of the city were a shambles. The day after the blackout, one policeman remembered finding "a shopping cart standing on the sidewalk, and across the top was this huge, five-foot-long side of beef still mostly frozen. It was as if the guy who'd stolen it suddenly said to himself, 'What the [heck] am I doing with this?' and so he left it there."[1]

In Bushwick, Brooklyn, two blocks of buildings had gone up in flames after two four-story buildings and a large department store burned to the ground. The elevated subway line on Broadway was shut down for fear that the fire-damaged buildings lining the tracks would collapse on the trains.[2]

Nearly four thousand people were arrested in New York City during the blackout. Thousands more escaped. Damages to businesses, private homes, and government agencies were estimated to be as high as $1 billion. New York City and Westchester County were declared disaster areas so that they could begin receiving federal money to recover. City officials estimated that during the blackout, 418 police officers and 59 firefighters were injured. More than 67,000 emergency calls were received (about four times the normal number), and 1,037 fires were set. So many false alarms were called in that no one was able to keep track of them.[3]

"I felt really bad for the city that night," a patrolman in the West Bronx would later say of the blackout. "I was standing there watching . . .

Fires started during the 1977 blackout can be seen raging in Brooklyn in this aerial photo.

and it was eating the heart out of me. The people were so stupid—they didn't see they were only hurting themselves."[4] Psychologist Morton Bard of the Graduate Center of New York's City University observed that the looting "had a quality of madness. I cannot believe that they cleaned out a store of prayer shawls and Bibles."[5]

*B*roken mannequins and shattered glass litter the floor of this clothing store in the wake of the 1977 blackout.

Miguel Ten, a Vietnam veteran, had stood guard at Arnet's Children's Wear store during the blackout. He noted that the conditions "[reminded] me of Pleiku in 1966. There was a war out here. And the mannequins remind me of the dead people I saw in Nam without legs and arms."[6]

One of the major differences between the 1965 and 1977 blackouts concerned the utility companies' safety and backup measures. Prior to the 1965 blackout, the United States had experienced a boom in housing, office space, and factory construction during the 1950s. This growth brought increased demand for electricity. In order to provide more efficient service, public-utility companies banded together to form power networks, or "grids." These grids connected power stations in one company's area of service with those in other areas by means of high-voltage power transmission lines.

Two power grids covered the densely populated northeastern U.S. and southeastern Canada. One was the Canada-United States Eastern (CANUSE) Interconnection. This covered Ontario, the New England states, and

New York State. The other was the Pennsylvania-New Jersey-Maryland (PJM) Interconnection. Both grids are still in place today.

The power grid idea had a major flaw, however. The main problem was that the systems did not have enough measures in place to prevent unexpected power overloads at certain key points. This is what happened in 1965, when a relay at an Ontario power station touched off overloads on transmission lines in the CANUSE and PJM grids. Human error was also responsible in part for that blackout. Some years earlier, that relay was set to trip (go offline) when the electricity transmitted went above

*R*avaged Harlem storefronts are shown here in the aftermath of the 1977 blackout.

375,000 volts—even though the line could actually transmit up to 500,000 volts.

Until the Great Northeast Blackout of 1965, most Americans were not aware that power grids connected them with far-flung places like Canada. In the aftermath of the outage, many politicians and newspaper editors pointed out the dangers of establishing closely connected grids. They thought it was dangerous that a single relay switch could cause a massive blackout. An editorial in *The New York Times* argued that the idea of a power grid was "far from foolproof" and warned that "until the weaknesses in this system can be discovered and corrected, the nation remains dangerously vulnerable" to suffering another major blackout.[8]

On July 10, 1977, Con Ed chairman Charles Luce appeared before the U.S. House of Representatives to speak to the Subcommittee on Energy and Power. He proudly "guaranteed" that there was no chance of another widespread power outage like that of 1965. When a blackout struck three days later, people wondered what Luce must have been thinking to offer such a promise.

In many ways, the causes of the 1977 blackout were the opposite of those that launched the 1965 blackout. In the first crisis, the grids may have been too tightly connected. In the second one, it appeared that the New York area was not connected closely enough to the CANUSE grid.

In 1977, the New York area still relied on a narrow corridor (passageway) of power transmission that ran through Westchester County. It was also connected to the PJM grid farther south. But on July 13, 1977, three power plants on this southern grid were shut down with mechanical problems. This meant that Con Ed's system was generating much less power than it normally would. With temperatures in the mid-90s, the area was using huge amounts of electricity because of all the air conditioners that were running. New York was relying on the Westchester County transmission line alone to supply an extra 2 million kilowatts of electricity to make up for the failed power stations to the south.

It was the worst time ever for a thunderstorm, but one rolled through Westchester County that evening. Con Ed claimed that their power transmission lines running from Indian Point 3 nuclear power plant were struck by lightning multiple times, causing an overload.[9] As a result, the circuit breakers designed to isolate (close off) the overload malfunctioned. Instead of keeping the over- load within a small area, the faulty circuit breakers allowed the overload to move southward. Con Ed station

Con Ed Chairman Charles Luce responds to reporters' questions during a press conference on Thursday, July 14, 1977.

operators saw that this was happening and tried to keep the blackout from spreading. In the confusion and panic, however, they failed to do so. As a result, automatic safety systems kicked in—the same ones that were created after the 1965 blackout. This actually helped spread the blackout over a greater area.[10]

New York's financial losses from the July 1977 blackout were staggering. Not surprisingly, many people—including Mayor Abe Beame—blamed Con Ed. "Con Ed's performance is, at the very best, gross negligence," the mayor said, "and at the worst, far more serious."[11]

In response to the criticism, Con Ed announced that it would take "super-extra precautionary measures" to keep another blackout from occurring. It installed more backup generators and increased staffing. The company also said it would train plant operators more thoroughly and would better manage the Energy Control Center, whose members made emergency decisions. Many were skeptical, however. Some thought that the improvements were promised to restore the public's confidence and avoid losing money for the company.[12]

One thing that seemed almost impossible to repair was New York City's reputation. Across the country, residents of other cities wondered whether such a disaster could happen where they lived. Most believed that even if the power were to go out, their cities would not explode into rioting. They were certain that such chaos could only occur in a city as "broken down" as New York. In Washington, D.C., the *Post* and the *Star* both ran the story on front pages, emphasizing the looting and vandalism.[13]

Three months after the blackout, President Jimmy Carter visited the devastated South Bronx. He was stunned by what he saw and he pledged federal assistance. New York City's government also declared that it was developing a strategy to repair the city's problems and bring it out of financial distress.

Later that year, Congress passed the Community Reinvestment Act (CRA) as the first step in President Carter's new urban policy. This anti-redlining law, which took effect in 1979, pressured banks to invest in urban neighborhoods. Such measures greatly aided in New York City's recovery. It would take many years, however, for New Yorkers and other Americans to see the results.

*P*resident Jimmy Carter visited the South Bronx three months after the 1977 blackout and pledged federal assistance to the city.

CHAPTER 5

"Never Say Never"

Can a power failure like the 1977 blackout happen again? In the decades since it occurred, utility companies, city officials, and power customers across the country have asked themselves this question.

In December 1998, San Francisco, California, suffered a widespread blackout when a construction crew's error caused a blowout at a Pacific Gas & Electric power station. Almost one million people in a forty-nine-square-mile area were without power for seven hours. Mayor Willie Brown declared a state of emergency during the blackout, but no accidents, lootings, or injuries were reported. Brown explained that the reasons for the calm had to do with the city's history of earthquakes, and the careful planning that resulted. "All the rehearsals and all the preparations and all the trial runs [for earthquakes] have now paid [off]," he said after electricity was restored. "San Franciscans have been performing magnificently."[1]

The situation was very different in 1999, when

power outages throughout the East Coast left millions without power in more than 100-degree heat. The temperatures and lack of power contributed to seventeen deaths in New York, New Jersey, Pennsylvania, Massachusetts, and Illinois. In New York City, 680,000 Con Ed customers went without power, forcing some to sleep outdoors on sidewalks to get relief from the stifling heat inside their homes. Although only a few attempted break-ins and arrests were reported, Mayor Rudy Giuliani was furious over the outages and compared them to the 1977 blackout: "This is the greatest city in the world,

New York City Mayor Rudolph Giuliani addresses the media on July 7, 1999, in the wake of several massive power outages.

and we shouldn't be living on the brink of blackouts when its gets hot out," he fumed. "That's like living on the brink of bankruptcy like we used to live on, and there is no reason for it."[2]

A great deal has changed in the energy industry since the New York City blackout of 1977. One of the biggest changes is deregulation. Beginning in the 1980s, many people in the electricity business, as well as Congress and the federal government, were calling for more competition in the industry. They believed that until that time, most power companies operated almost as monopolies— meaning they had complete control over the supply of electricity in their markets. They wanted to open up the markets to competition.

In 1992, the U.S. Congress passed the National Energy Policy Act, which required power producers to compete with one another to sell electricity to public utilities. Four years later, the Federal Energy Regulatory Commission (FERC) ordered utilities to open their transmission lines to competitors. Six states started pilot (test) programs that allowed competition: New Hampshire, Arizona, California, Massachusetts, Rhode Island, and Pennsylvania.[3]

In Pennsylvania, which launched its program in 1998, deregulation has been largely successful. According to newspaper reports in October 1999, about 500,000 consumers had already switched to different utility companies. That number was more than 10 percent of the state's population. Philadelphia-area residents who switched to a cheaper provider discovered that they saved an average of $120 per year.[4]

In California, however, even some who supported deregulation changed their minds after electricity prices began to rise. By 1998, two years after the state enacted its deregulation plan, consumer groups tried unsuccessfully to bring up a vote that would cancel the plan. In the

*U*niversity of California student Jesse Sisgold is helped out of an elevator that stalled between floors during one of the rolling blackouts that struck California on January 17, 2001.

summer of 2000, the price of electricity in California skyrocketed. The state needed more and more power for computers, appliances, networks, and communication systems. Some Californians watched their electricity bills double, as suppliers from outside the state took advantage of the electricity shortage and charged whatever they could get. That winter, prices continued to rise, and parts of the state experienced periodic blackouts as energy shortages occurred.

In early 2002, evidence came to light that these blackouts may have been the result of devious practices by some energy companies taking advantage of deregulation. Internal memos from the Enron Corporation

*F*ormer Chief Executive Officer of Enron Kenneth Lay is pictured here on April 7, 2000. Enron's illegal business practices may have contributed to the rolling blackouts that plagued California throughout 2000 and 2001.

described several different strategies the company used to manipulate the energy market and fleece money from consumers. These schemes were given nick-names, such as "Ricochet," in which Enron would buy power in California, send it out of state on a regional grid, then sell it back to California at a higher price. In another strategy called "Death Star," Enron created the illusion of congestion on California's power grid and then got paid by the state to relieve this false congestion. Such practices cost California con-sumers tens of billions of dollars. In May 2002, compa-ny lawyers for Enron admitted that these practices "may have contributed" to the state's severe power shortages and blackouts.[5]

These strategies were some of the many questionable practices conducted by Enron. The company also engaged in deceptive accounting, which misled employees and shareholders about the company's worth. As these scan-dals came to light, Enron stock plummeted. Ranked the seventh-largest company in the U.S. in terms of revenue in 2000, Enron was forced to file for bankruptcy in December 2001. This was the largest bankruptcy in U.S. history at the time. Company shareholders lost billions of dollars. Thousands of employees lost their jobs.

The fall of Enron also cast suspicion on other energy companies operating in California. Those companies with big stakes in the California market soon suffered financially as their stock prices dropped sharply. Some fell by as much as 33 percent in just over a month.[6]

Today, twenty-five states are in the process of deregulating electricity. But the energy crisis in California has had a great impact. At least two states, Nevada and Arkansas, have decided to suspend their deregulation programs. They are carefully watching how California handles the problems in its own program.

In light of the difficulties with deregulation, power company officials no longer make the kind of promises that Con Ed chairman Charles Luce made in July 1977—that another massive blackout could not happen. "We have a saying in this business," said Charlie Durkin, a Con Ed representative. "We never say never."[7]

Chapter 1. Terror in the Darkness

1. Frank Merrick, "Night of Terror," *TIME*, July 25, 1977, Vol. 110, No. 4, p. 22.

2. Ibid.

3. Ralph Blumenthal, "No Panic Reported in Subways Among Trapped Passengers," *The New York Times*, July 14, 1977, p. A.

4. Robert Curvin and Bruce Porter, *Blackout Looting!: New York City, July 13, 1977* (New York: Gardner Press, Inc., 1979), p. 3.

5. Ibid., pp. 44, 39, 9.

6. Ibid., p. 15.

7. Selwyn Raab, "Ravage Continues Far Into Day; Gunfire and Bottles Beset Police," *The New York Times*, July 15, 1977, p. A3.

8. Lawrence Van Gelder, "Power Failure Blacks Out New York; Thousands Trapped in the Subways; Looters and Vandals Hit Some Areas; State Troopers Sent Into City As Crime Rises," *The New York Times*, July 14, 1977, p. A.

9. Raab, "Ravage Continues," p. A3.

10. Judith Cummings, "Store-Pillaging Unchecked in Two Brooklyn Sections," *The New York Times*, July 15, 1977, p. A3.

11. Ibid.

Chapter 2. A City in Distress

1. Center for History and New Media (CHNM), George Mason University, "Events/1965: Great Northeast Blackout," *The Blackout History Project: New York City 1965/1977*, June 27, 2000, <http://blackout.gmu.edu/events/tl1965.html> (June 5, 2002).

2. Clyde Haberman, "Surviving Fiscal Ruin (And Disco)," *New York Times on the Web: NYC 100*, January 25, 1998, <http://www.nytimes.com/learning/general/specials/nyc100/nyc100-8-haberman.html> (June 5, 2002).

3. Ibid.

4. Haberman, "Surviving Fiscal Ruin (And Disco)," and Brockman, Richard, "Notes While Being Hijacked," *Atlantic Monthly*, December 1976, Vol. 238(6), p. 68, <http://www.theatlantic.com/issues/76dec/brockman.htm> (June 5, 2002).

5. Leonard Levitt, "Won't Let Me Stop Killing: Terrified Couples Shunned NYC Lovers' Lanes Until a Parking Ticket Ended Son of Sam's Reign," *Long Island: Our History*, n.d., <http://www.lihistory.com/9/hs9sam.htm> (June 5, 2002).

6. Ibid.

Chapter 3. The Long, Dark Hours

1. Eric Pace, "A Grim Game of Cat and Mouse on Tour of East Harlem." *The New York Times*, July 15, 1977, p. A5.

2. Robert Curvin and Bruce Porter, *Blackout Looting!: New York City, July 13, 1977* (New York: Gardner Press, Inc., 1979), p. 41.

3. Charlayne Hunter Gault, "When Poverty's Part of Life, Looting is Not Condemned," *The New York Times*, July 15, 1977, p. A4.

4. Judith Cummings, "Store-Pillaging Unchecked in Two Brooklyn Sections," *The New York Times*, July 15, 1977, p. A3.

5. Lawrence Van Gelder, "Power Failure Blacks Out New York; Thousands Trapped in the Subways; Looters and Vandals Hit Some Areas; State Troopers Sent Into City As Crime Rises," *The New York Times*, July 14, 1977, p. A.

6. Cynthia Tornquist, "After 20 Years, New Yorkers Recall Night the Lights Went Out," *CNN.com*, July 12, 1997, <http://www.cnn.com/US/9707/12/blackout/> (June 5, 2002).

7. Center for History and New Media (CHNM), George Mason University, "Events/1965: Great Northeast Blackout," *The Blackout History Project: New York City 1965/1977*, June 27, 2000, <http://blackout.gmu.edu/events/tl1965.html> (June 5, 2002).

8. Curvin and Porter, pp. 8, 12.

9. Lawrence K. Altman, "Bellevue Patients Resuscitated with Hand-Squeezed Air Bags," *The New York Times*, July 14, 1977, p. A1.

10. Lawrence K. Altman, "Inquiry is Slated Into Two Deaths At Bellevue Hospital in Blackout," *The New York Times*, July 15, 1977, p. A10.

11. Ibid.

12. John T. McQuiston, "Medical Center's Parking Lot Like War Zone Field Hospital," *The New York Times*, July 15, 1977, p. A10.

13. Selwyn Raab, "Ravage Continues Far Into Day; Gunfire and Bottles Beset Police," *The New York Times*, July 15, 1977, p. A3.

14. Curvin and Porter, pp. 43, 41.

15. Ralph Blumenthal, "Subways and Suburban Railroads Out of Service for Most of the Day," *The New York Times*, July 15, 1977, p. A10.

16. Deirdre Carmody, "Some Led Others by Flashlight, Others Knocked on Doors to Help," *The New York Times*, July 14, 1977, p. B.

Chapter 4. Learning Lessons

1. Robert Curvin and Bruce Porter, *Blackout Looting!: New York City, July 13, 1977* (New York: Gardner Press, Inc., 1979), p. 45.

2. Ibid., pp. 135–136.

3. Robert D. McFadden, "'Disaster' Status Given New York and Westchester to Speed Loans; Services Resume After Blackout," *The New York Times*, July 16, 1977, p. A1.

4. Curvin and Porter, p. 81.

5. Frederic Golden, "Looking for a Reason," *TIME*, July 25, 1977, Vol. 110, No. 4, p. 17.

6. Frank Merrick, "Night of Terror," *TIME*, July 25, 1977, Vol. 110, No. 4, p. 12.

7. Center for History and New Media (CHNM), George Mason University, "Events/1965: Great Northeast Blackout," *The Blackout History Project: New York City 1965/1977*, June 27, 2000, <http://blackout.gmu.edu/events/tl1965.html> (June 5, 2002).

8. Wade Roush, "The Precious Dark: The Great New York City Blackouts of 1965 and 1977," *The Machine Stops: The Making and the Meanings of Catastrophic Technological Failures*, n.d., <http://home.earthlink.net/~wroush/disasters/black0.html> (June 5, 2002), and Charles D. Sigwart, "The Great Northeast Blackout of 1965," *Disasters*, n.d., <http://www.ceet.niu.edu/faculty/vanmeer/outage.htm> (June 5, 2002).

9. Victor K. McElheny, "Improbable Strikes by Lightning Tripped Its System, Con Ed Says," *The New York Times*, July 15, 1977, p. A2.

10. Roush and Sigwart.

11. Frank Merrick, "Night of Terror," p. 12.

12. Roush and Sigwart.

13. Michael Sterne, "Nation's Reaction to the Blackout: Yawns to 'Could It Happen Here?'," *The New York Times*, July 15, 1977, p. A9.

Chapter 5. "Never Say Never"

1. Don Knapp, "'Simple Human Error' Blamed for San Francisco Blackout," *CNN.com*, December 9, 1998, <http://www.cnn.com/US/9812/08/sanfran.blackout.02/> (June 5, 2002).

2. "Heat Wave Eases; New York, Other Cities Plagued by Blackouts," *CNN.com*, July 7, 1999, <http://www.cnn.com/WEATHER/9907/07/heat.wave.01/index.html> (June 5, 2002).

3. Center for Responsive Politics, "Electricity Deregulation," *OpenSecrets.org*, January 30, 2001, <http://www.opensecrets.org/news/electricity.htm> (June 5, 2002).

4. Ibid.

5. Richard A. Oppel, Jr., and Jeff Gerth, "Enron Forced Up California Prices, Documents Show," *The New York Times*, May 7, 2002, p. A1.

6. Chris Taylor, "California Scheming," *TIME*, May 20, 2002, p. 42.

7. Cynthia Tornquist, "After 20 Years, New Yorkers Recall Night the Lights Went Out," *CNN.com*, July 12, 1997, <http://www.cnn.com/US/9707/12/blackout/> (June 5, 2002).

Glossary

bedlam—A place or scene of uproar and confusion.

commissioner—An official in charge of a government department.

deregulation—The act of allowing companies in a certain industry or market to compete for customers rather than have one company control all goods or services.

inflation—A continual increase in the prices of goods and services.

kilowatt—A metric unit that measures electrical power.

laceration—A torn and ragged wound.

monopoly—A commercial product or service controlled by one person or company; or having complete control over the entire supply of goods or a service in a certain market.

public utility—A business organization (such as an electric company) that performs a public service and must follow special government regulations.

redlining—The banking practice of denying home-loan funds to residents of poor inner-city neighborhoods.

relay—A device that opens or closes a circuit that in turn operates another device (such as a switch in another circuit).

revenue—The income that a government collects.

sniper—A person who shoots at exposed people from a concealed place.

transformer—A device for changing an electric current into one of different voltage.

transmission—The passage of electricity in the space between power stations.

urban—Relating to or typical of a city.

volt—A unit that measures the potential for energy to travel from one point to another.

vulnerable—Open to attack or damage.

Further Reading

Brown, Paul. *Energy and Resources.* Danbury, Conn.: Franklin Watts, 1998.

Bryce, Robert. *Pipe Dreams: Greed, Ego, and the Death of Enron.* New York: Public Affairs, 2002.

Feinstein, Stephen. *The 1970s: From Watergate to Disco.* Berkeley Heights, N.J.: Enslow Publishers, Inc., 2000.

Grossman, Peter Z. *In Came the Darkness: The Story of Blackouts.* New York: Simon & Schuster Children's Publishing, 1984.

McLeish, Ewan. *Energy Resources: Our Impact on the Planet.* Austin, Tex.: Raintree Steck-Vaughn Publishers, 2002.

Internet Addresses

The Blackout History Project: New York City 1965/1977
http://chnm.gmu.edu/blackout/main.html

After 20 Years, New Yorkers Recall Night the Lights Went Out
http://www.cnn.com/US/9707/12/blackout/

PBS Frontline: Blackout
http://www.pbs.org/wgbh/pages/frontline/shows/blackout/

Protection Against Power Disruptions
http://www.powerprotectiononline.org/